W9-BRS-527

ideals®
LIBERTY

"Here on this spot was born a nation that will be
  Adept in all the humanities. Spreading in circles, as when
A pebble is thrown into a morning lake,
  Its concepts will cover a continent with a vision of dignity
At last made real. Here a race of men will evolve
  That will instruct the world in justice and in love.
A race of men to whom the entire world is a religion,
  Whose vessels, laden with much more than cargoes,
Will pass through the seven oceans, bearing with them
  The beliefs of all our countries, all our hearts."

Harry Brown

ISBN 0-8249-1032-X 350

Publisher, Patricia A. Pingry
Editor/Ideals, Kathleen S. Pohl
Managing Editor, Marybeth Owens
Photographic Editor, Gerald Koser
Staff Artist, Patrick McRae
Research Editor, Linda Robinson
Typesetter, Kim Kaczanowski
Art Intern, Cindy Hepp

IDEALS — Vol. 42, No. 1 December MCMLXXXIV IDEALS (ISSN 0019-137X) is published eight times a year.
February, March, May, June, August, September, November, December
by IDEALS PUBLISHING CORPORATION, 11315 Watertown Plank Road, Milwaukee, Wis. 53226
Second class postage paid at Milwaukee, Wisconsin and additional mailing offices.
Copyright © MCMLXXXIV by IDEALS PUBLISHING CORPORATION.
POSTMASTER: Send address changes to Ideals, Post Office Box 2100, Milwaukee, Wis. 53201
All rights reserved. Title IDEALS registered U.S. Patent Office.
Published simultaneously in Canada.

SINGLE ISSUE — $3.50
ONE YEAR SUBSCRIPTION — eight consecutive issues as published — $15.95
TWO YEAR SUBSCRIPTION — sixteen consecutive issues as published — $27.95
Outside U.S.A., add $4.00 per subscription year for postage and handling

The cover and entire contents of IDEALS are fully protected by copyright and must
not be reproduced in any manner whatsoever. Printed and bound in U.S.A.

*Front and
back covers
THE CAPITOL
Gene Ahrens*

The New World

This America is an ancient land,
Conquered and re-conquered by successive races.
It is the Radiant Land and Continent of the Blest
Forever won and forever lost,
And forever seen by that vision which thrilled Balboa
Staring the Pacific;
And forever seen by that revelation of the soul
Which came to John Keats through Homer,
For both seas and land, and visions of a new day
   may be seen,
And gold may be seen by Cortes and Pizarro
   and their sons,
Who turn all Radiant Lands to gold, and starve therefore.
But this New World is forever new to hands
   that keep it new.

Edgar Lee Masters

Photo opposite
ELIZABETH II
16th Century Reproduction
Fred Sieb

The New Nation

On — on to where the tea-ships ride!
　And now their ranks are forming —
A rush, and up the Dartmouth's side
　The Mohawk band is swarming!
See the fierce natives! What a glimpse
　Of paint and fur and feather,
As all at once the full grown imps
　Light on the deck together!
A scarf the pigtail's secret keeps,
　A blanket hides the breeches —
And out the cursed cargo leaps,
　And overboard it pitches!

O woman, at the evening board
　So gracious, sweet, and purring,
So happy while the tea is poured,
　So blest while spoons are stirring,
What martyr can compare with thee,
　The mother, wife, or daughter,
That night, instead of best Bohea,
　Condemned to milk and water!
Ah, little dreams the quiet dame
　Who plies with rock and spindle
The patient flax, how great a flame
　Yon little spark shall kindle!

The lurid morning shall reveal
　A fire no king can smother
Where British flint and Boston steel
　Have clashed against each other!
Old charters shrivel in its track,
　His Worship's bench has crumbled,
It climbs and clasps the union-jack,
　Its blazoned pomp is humbled,
The flags go down on land and sea
　Like corn before the reapers;
So burned the fire that brewed the tea
　That Boston served her keepers!

The waves that wrought a century's wreck
　Have rolled o'er Whig and Tory;
The Mohawks on the Dartmouth's deck
　Still live in song and story;
The waters in the rebel bay
　Have kept the tea-leaf savor;
Our old North-Enders in their spray
　Still taste a Hyson flavor;
And Freedom's teacup still o'erflows
　With ever fresh libations,
To cheat of slumber all her foes
　And cheer the wakening nations!

Oliver Wendell Holmes

VALLEY FORGE by Oscar de Mejo, acrylic on canvas, 26 x 36, Aberbach Fine Art, New York, New York (from the book MY AMERICA published by Harry Abrams Inc.).

The Horse's Version of Paul Revere's Ride

Listen, my jockeys, and you shall hear
How I carried my master, Paul Revere,
From the Charles bank, at the midnight hour,
When the lights flashed out in the belfry tower.
The British had landed! Paul gave me a pat
And said, "Well, Bess, old gal that's that."

And off we sped through the country wide —
And maybe I didn't give Paul a ride!
But honest, I had to laugh at the folk
We waked, who said, "What's this, a joke?"
And one old party, a Cambridge squire,
In nightgown and helmet, yelled, "Where's the fire?"

And of course, as I couldn't talk, you know,
I just whinnied, "You tell 'em Paul; let's go!"
Then away we flew, through village and town.
I don't know the route but it's all set down
In Longfellow's poem, I simply said:
"We'll make the grade if I don't drop dead."

Well, I didn't and when that ride was done,
And Paul said, "Bess, there's Lexington,"
And I saw a stall and a pile of hay,
Well, I just lay down and I passed away.
And when I woke up next day and heard
What the minutemen had done — my word!
I wobbled up and gave three horse cheers
For that ride of mine — and Paul Revere's!

Author Unknown

from
The Declaration of Independence

When, in the Course of human events, it becomes necessary for one people to dissolve the political bands which have connected them with another, and to assume, among the Powers of the earth, the separate and equal station to which the Laws of Nature and of Nature's God entitle them, a decent respect to the opinions of mankind requires that they should declare the causes which impel them to the separation.

We hold these truths to be self-evident: that all men are created equal; that they are endowed by their Creator with certain inalienable Rights; that among these are Life, Liberty, and the Pursuit of Happiness. That, to secure these Rights, Governments are instituted among Men, deriving their just powers from the consent of the governed. That, whenever any Form of Government becomes destructive of these ends, it is the Right of the People to alter or to abolish it, and to institute new Government, laying its foundation on such Principles, and organizing its Powers in such form, as to them shall seem most likely to effect their Safety and Happiness.

Photo opposite
DRAFTING THE DECLARATION
OF INDEPENDENCE
J. L. G. Ferris
(Photo, Three Lions)

Betsy Ross

She was five and twenty; the chisel of life
Had graved old lines on her girlish brow.
She had watched and waited, a soldier's wife,
A soldier's widow she sorrowed now.
Day by day, as her slim hands flew
Backward and forward weaving lace,
She counted the dark things fate can do;
Then — a light began in the dusky place.

This is the way the light began:
A sudden shadow was on the floor;
She turned and fronted a martial man
Gaunt and courteous in the door,
General Washington, come to say
He knew her skill and her needle's grace.
Would she make a flag for America?
A beauty broke in her wistful face,

A shining caught her . . . . They shaped and planned,
The tall man towering to the beams,
The young lace maker; for one dear land
They wove and worked in a mist of dreams.
Six white bands and seven bright bars —
Eager they watched the pattern come —
A fair blue field and a welter of stars,
Glory gathering in the gloom.

Hour by hour, left alone,
Singing she wrought for far-off years,
Fadeless color to stitch upon,
Starry stuff for her valiant shears;
Fretting no longer of fate and doom,
She labored loving, till free and high,
The light that had kindled in one small room
Flamed to the world in a nation's sky!

                                    Nancy Byrd Turner

From ONE THOUSAND AMERICAN THINGS, copyright 1949, 1956 by the Spencer Press,
Inc., courtesy of Melvin Lee Steadman, Jr.

INDEPENDENCE BELL

There was tumult in the city,
   In the quaint old Quaker town,
And the streets were thronged with people
   Passing restless up and down —
People gathering at the corners,
   Where they whispered lip to ear,
While the sweat stood on their temples,
   With the stress of hope and fear.

As the bleak Atlantic currents
   Lash the wild Newfoundland shore,
So they beat about the State House,
   So they surged against the door;
And the mingling of their voices
   Swelled in harmony profound,
Till the quiet street of Chestnut
   Was all turbulent with sound.

"Will they do it?" "Dare they do it?"
   "Who is speaking?" "What's the news?"
"What of Adams?" "What of Sherman?"
   "Oh, God grant they won't refuse!"
"Make some way, there!" "Let me nearer!"
   "I am stifling!" "Stifle then!
When a nation's life's at hazard
   We've no time to think of men!"

So they surged against the State House,
   While all solemnly inside
Sat the Continental Congress,
   Truth and reason for their guide;
O'er a simple scroll debating:
   Which, though simple it might be,
Yet should shake the cliffs of England
   With the thunders of the free.

Far aloft in the high steeple
   Sat the bellman, old and gray;
He was weary of the tyrant
   And his iron-sceptered sway.
So he sat with one hand ready
   On the clapper of the bell,
Till his eye should catch the signal,
   The expected news to tell.

See! See! the dense crowd quivers
   As beside the door a boy
Looks forth with hands uplifted,
   His eyes alight with joy.
Hushed the people's swelling murmur
   As they listen breathlessly —
"Ring!" he shouts. "Ring, Grandpapa!
   Ring! oh, ring for liberty!"

Quickly at the welcome signal
   The old bellman lifts his hand;
Forth he sends the good news, making
   Iron music through the land.
How they shouted! What rejoicing!
   How the old bell shook the air,
Till the clang of freedom echoed
   From the belfries everywhere.

The old State House bell is silent,
   Hushed is now its clamorous tongue,
But the spirit it awakened
   Still is living, ever young.
And we'll ne'er forget the bellman
   Who, that great day in July,
Hailed the birth of Independence,
   Which, please God, shall never die.

Photo opposite
LIBERTY BELL
K. Rodko
(Photo, Three Lions)

Author Unknown

All-American Desserts

County Fair Candied Apples

10 to 15 medium-sized apples
3 cups sugar
¼ teaspoon cream of tartar

⅔ cup water
1 teaspoon lemon juice
1 to 2 teaspoons red food coloring

Wash and dry apples. Skewer stem end of apples. Combine sugar, cream of tartar, water, and lemon juice in heavy saucepan; stir constantly over low heat until sugar dissolves. Add food coloring. Boil, without stirring, until mixture reaches the hard-crack stage (until temperature registers 300° F. on candy thermometer). Remove from heat. Immediately submerge apples in syrup; twist quickly. Place on buttered cookie sheet. Serve same day as prepared.

Martha's Cherry Crumble

2½ cups fresh red cherries
2½ cups crushed pineapple, drained
1½ cups white sugar
⅓ cup quick tapioca
1 cup bran flakes
1 cup quick oats
2 cups sifted flour
1 cup brown sugar
¼ teaspoon salt
1 teaspoon baking soda
¾ cup butter, melted
1½ teaspoons vanilla
Whipped cream, optional
Fresh cherries, optional

To make fruit sauce, cook cherries, pineapple, white sugar, and tapioca over medium heat, about 5 minutes, until mixture thickens. Set aside. In large bowl, crumble together dry ingredients. Add butter and vanilla and stir with fork. Press two-thirds of dry crumble mixture in bottom of 9 x 13-inch greased casserole dish. Add cherry-pineapple mixture. Top with remainder of crumble mixture. Bake at 375° F. for 30 minutes. Remove from oven. Cool. Let stand overnight. Garnish with cherries and whipped cream, if desired.

Yankee Doodle Dandy Pie

1 package (3¼ ounces) vanilla pudding mix
2 cups milk
1 package (8 ounces) cream cheese, softened
½ teaspoon vanilla
1 8-inch prepared graham cracker piecrust
20 to 25 strawberries, hulled
1 pint blueberries
Whipped cream or other topping, optional

Combine pudding mix and 2 cups of milk in saucepan. Bring to full boil over medium heat, stirring constantly. Remove from heat. Add cream cheese and stir until smooth. Add vanilla. Let mixture cool for 5 minutes, stirring twice. Pour pudding mixture into graham cracker crust. Refrigerate 3 hours or overnight. Place strawberries in circle around outer edge of pie. Put 1 large strawberry in center of pie. Place blueberries over remaining pudding surface (see photo opposite). Serve with whipped cream or other topping, if desired.

Photo opposite
ALL-AMERICAN DESSERTS
Gerald Koser

America's First Ladies

As ambassadors of the heart and hearth, first ladies have always played an important (albeit an oftentimes behind-the-scenes) role in the history of presidential leadership in this country.

Martha Dandridge Custis Washington was truly a pioneer in the role as first lady. The young Widow Custis married George Washington, the dashing soldier from Virginia, in 1759. During the next sixteen years she performed traditional motherly and wifely duties of the time — gardening, sewing, weaving, cooking, and supervising slaves on the 8,000-acre Mount Vernon estate.

The serenity of Mount Vernon life was disrupted with the outbreak of the Revolutionary War in 1775 when George Washington was called upon to serve as commander in chief of the Continental Army. Martha remained at Mount Vernon, dutifully overseeing the affairs of the estate. During the eight long years of war, she made many trips to the battlefield, visiting her husband at various camp headquarters, caring for the sick, and cheering the soldiers at the front lines.

At the end of the war, George returned to the tranquility of Mount Vernon for a short time, before being called upon once again by his country—this time to serve as president of the newly-founded nation. Although she treasured the serenity and privacy of Mount Vernon life, Martha rose again to the occasion and accompanied her husband, first to New York, and later to the new capital in Philadelphia, as George served two terms in office. Ever adaptable and always willing to put her husband's political responsibilities first, Martha proved to be a dignified and gracious hostess as first lady, setting a fine example for all first ladies who followed.

Dolley Payne Todd Madison has often been described as the most popular first lady. Although of Quaker upbringing, the beautiful, vivacious Dolley had no trouble adapting to the social responsibilities of political life. While her husband, James, served as secretary of state during the Jefferson administration, Dolley assumed the role of hostess to the nation, a role gratefully acknowledged by the widowed Thomas Jefferson. On special occasions, Dolley opened the President's House to the public and won the hearts of the American people. Indeed, history suggests that Dolley Madison's charm may well have been largely responsible for James Madison's election to the presidency in 1809.

But Dolley was soon to be credited with more than just beauty and charm. In 1814 when the British invaded Washington, she proved to be coolheaded, courageous and resourceful in time of danger. In her husband's absence, she collected invaluable records, the original Declaration of Independence, and an original Stuart portrait of George Washington; she and her servants escaped with the valuables, barely ahead of the oncoming British troops. The President's House was destroyed by the fire. It was Dolley who persuaded her husband to re-establish the capital in Washington, rather than moving the seat of government back to Philadelphia. Three years later a new Executive Mansion was built on the site of the original. The blackened walls were painted white to cover traces of the fire. People began referring to it as "The White House." And Dolley Madison continued to exert her influence in the social and political life of the nation's capital.

Probably no one was a more unlikely candidate for her role as first lady than Anna Eleanor Roosevelt. A painfully shy, awkward little girl with braces on her teeth and noticeably poor posture, she shunned social events throughout her adolescent years. In 1905 she married Franklin D. Roosevelt, a distant cousin, and shortly thereafter was forced into a whirlwind of social activity as her husband served in a variety of public offices including state senator, assistant secretary of the navy, governor of New York, and finally, president of the United States.

In 1921 Franklin Roosevelt was stricken with infantile paralysis; he suffered the effects of the disease, in varying degrees, for the rest of his life. Eleanor became both his shield and his sword. She worked tirelessly to keep in touch with the American people, travelling long distances to stay informed on various political and social events, making public speeches in her husband's behalf, devoting tremendous amounts of time and energy to her children, and remaining her husband's constant caretaker and companion.

Eleanor Roosevelt was the first president's wife to devote herself to a career of social reform and political activity, and the first to accept public office after leaving the White House. Following her husband's death in 1945, Eleanor was appointed U.S. representative in the General Assembly of the United Nations, and later became chairman of the Human Rights Commission. The quiet, introspective little girl had become the selfless, energetic campaigner for human rights and gained world-wide respect in the process.

Amelia Rogers

Western Star

Americans are always moving on.
It's an old Spanish custom gone astray,
A sort of English fever, I believe,
Or just a mere desire to take French leave,
I couldn't say. I couldn't really say.
But, when the whistle blows, they go away.
Sometimes there never was a whistle blown,
But they don't care, for they can blow their own
Whistles of willow-stick and rabbit-bone,
Quail-calling through the rain
A dozen tunes but only one refrain,
"We don't know where we're going,
But we're on our way!"

* * * * *

Oh, paint your wagons with "Pike's Peak or Bust!"
Pack up the fiddle, rosin up the bow,
Vamoose, skedaddle, mosey, hit the grit!
(We pick our words, like nuggets, for the shine,
And, where they didn't fit, we make them fit,
Whittling a language out of birch and pine.)
We're off for Californ-iay,
We're off down the wild O-hi-o!
And every girl on Natchez bluff
Will cry as we go by-o!

* * * * *

Out of your fever and your moving on,
(Americans, Americans, Americans)
Out of your unassuaged and restless hearts,
Out of your conquest, out of your despair,
I make my song.

Stephen Vincent Benét

"WESTERN STAR" by Stephen Vincent Benet. Holt, Rinehart & Winston, Inc. Copyright, 1943 by Rosemary Carr Benet. Copyright renewed © 1971 by Rachel Benet Lewis, Thomas C. Benet & Stephanie Benet Mahin. Reprinted by permission of Brandt & Brandt Literary Agents Inc.

Photo opposite
CONESTOGA WAGON
Scotts Bluff, Nebraska
Jeff Gnass

The Pioneer
Woman
in the North Country

The eyes of the pioneer woman are blue, blue as the
   queen's velvet, clear as the skyey robes of
   Fra Angelico's angels.
There are no shadows in them.

Around us the country stretches, mile on mile, county on
   county, of wild unbroken ground.
Lakes are here, wide gray lakes that lie empty under the
   colorless sun of the north; and little familiar lakes,
   nestling among the trees.
Forests are here, scraggy, unkempt woods, too often
   lumbered, of jack-pine, scrub-oak and soft maple,
   choked with underbrush.
Wandering rutted roads are here, and untidy fences,
   shacks too quickly thrown together, and fields
   half-tilled.
At night the sun goes down in blood, loons cry across
   the lakes and far away the coyotes howl.
A strange land, a land half finished!

The forty acres of the pioneer are fifteen miles from town.
   Five miles away his nearest neighbor lives.
Yet the eyes of his wife are clear and unshadowed as
   emeralds in the sun.

"There are no blueberries this year or not enough to
   count," she says.
"I only put up forty quarts. . . ."

                             Eunice Tietjens

From PROFILES FROM HOME, by Eunice Tietjens. Copyright 1925 by Alfred A.
Knopf, Inc. and renewed 1953 by Cloyd Head. Reprinted by permission of the
publisher.

TOMBSTONE ARIZONA
—Josef Muench

Pioneers! O Pioneers!

Come my tan-faced children,
Follow well in order, get your weapons ready,
Have you your pistols? Have you your sharp-edged axes?
    Pioneers! O pioneers!

For we cannot tarry here,
We must march my darlings, we must bear the brunt of danger,
We the youthful sinewy races, all the rest on us depend,
    Pioneers! O pioneers!

O you youths, Western youths,
So impatient, full of action, full of manly pride and friendship,
Plain I see you Western youths, see you tramping with the foremost,
    Pioneers! O pioneers!

Have the elder races halted?
Do they droop and end their lesson, wearied over there beyond the sea?
We take up the task eternal, and the burden and the lesson,
    Pioneers! O pioneers!

All the past we leave behind,
We debouch upon a newer mightier world, varied world,
Fresh and strong the world we seize, world of labor and the march,
　　Pioneers! O pioneers!

　　We detachments steady throwing,
Down the edges, through the passes, up the mountain steep,
Conquering, holding, daring, venturing as we go the unknown ways,
　　Pioneers, O pioneers!

　　We primeval forests felling,
We the rivers stemming, vexing we and piercing deep the mines within,
We the surface broad surveying, we the virgin soil upheaving,
　　Pioneers! O pioneers!

　　Colorado men are we,
From the peaks gigantic, from the great sierras and the high plateaus,
From the mine and from the gully, from the hunting trail we come,
　　Pioneers! O pioneers!

　　From Nebraska, from Arkansas,
Central inland race are we, from Missouri, with the continental blood intervein'd,
All the hands of comrades clasping, all the Southern, all the Northern,
　　Pioneers! O pioneers!

Walt Whitman

Walthena

I turned my back when in the pot they tossed
My pewter spoons, to mold as shot for guns.
My mother owned a shelf of shining spoons and plates;
Can we have none but homemade wooden ones,
   Just handmade wooden ones?

I asked your father once if we might have
Crock plates to set our table. He said, "No,"
They dulled men's knives. So we must eat from plates
   of wood,
To keep knife-blades well sharpened against the foe,
   The ever-lurking foe.

Back home each Saturday my mother made
White candles, clean and straight. But out west here
Your father, laughing, scorns to make a candle mold,
When we have fatty pine-knots always near,
   Pine-knots and greasy bear-dips always near.

If I could hope some day to own a gown
Of smooth, fine store-cloth, little would I care
That I have only homespun linsey-woolsey now,
And shapeless shoepacks stiffed with moss to wear,
   Coarse, shapeless clothes to wear.

But though I could not own a pewter spoon nor store-
   cloth dress,
I snatched at least some beauty for my brood.
When pappy gave the boys their names, and I the girls,
He gave man-names that seemed like puncheons rude,
   Ax-hewn puncheons rude.

But I chose names for loveliness alone.
Fair-Anna is a spoon of silver bright,
Lizelle a silken gown, Morene a china bowl,
And you, Walthena, are a candle white,
   A tall, smooth candle white,
     Walthena.

Elisabeth Peck

From the book AMERICAN FRONTIER by Elisabeth Peck. Copyright © 1937, 1964 by Elisabeth Peck. Published by Doubleday and Co., Inc.

Photo opposite
ANTIQUE SPINNING WHEEL
James Tomasek
Cyr Color Photo Agency

Daniel Boone

Daniel Boone at twenty-one
Came with his tomahawk, knife and gun
Home from the French and Indian War
To North Carolina and the Yadkin shore.
He married his maid with a golden band,
Built his house and cleared his land;
But the deep woods claimed their son again
And he turned his face from the homes of men.
Over the Blue Ridge, dark and lone,
The Mountains of Iron, the Hills of Stone,
Braving the Shawnee's jealous wrath,
He made his way on the Warrior's Path.
Alone he trod the shadowed trails;
But he was the lord of a thousand vales
As he roved Kentucky, far and near,
Hunting the buffalo, elk and deer.
What joy to see, what joy to win
So fair a land for his kith and kin,
Of streams unstained and woods unhewn!
"Elbowroom!" laughed Daniel Boone.

From I SING THE PIONEER by Arthur Guiterman, published and copyrighted 1926 by
E. P. Dutton & Co., Inc. Reprinted by permission of Louise H. Sclove.

On the Wilderness Road that his axmen made
The settlers flocked to the first stockade;
The deerskin shirts and the coonskin caps
Filed through the glens and the mountain gaps;
And hearts were high in the fateful spring
When the land said "Nay!" to the stubborn king.
While the men of the East of farm and town
Strove with the troops of the British Crown,
Daniel Boone from a surge of hate
Guarded a nation's westward gate.

Down on the fort in a wave of flame
The Shawnee horde and the Mingo came,
And the stout logs shook in a storm of lead;
But Boone stood firm and the savage fled.
Peace! And the settlers flocked anew,
The farm lands spread, the town lands grew;
But Daniel Boone was ill at ease
When he saw the smoke in his forest trees.
"There'll be no game in the country soon.
Elbowroom!" cried Daniel Boone.

Straight as a pine at sixty-five —
Time enough for a man to thrive —
He launched his bateau on Ohio's breast
And his heart was glad as he oared it west;
There were kindly folk and his own true blood
Where great Missouri rolls his flood;
New woods, new streams and room to spare,
And Daniel Boone found comfort there.
Yet far he ranged toward the sunset still,
Where the Kansas runs and the Smoky Hill,

And the prairies toss, by the south wind blown;
And he killed his bear on the Yellowstone.
But ever he dreamed of new domains
With vaster woods and wider plains;
Ever he dreamed of a world-to-be
Where there are no bounds and the soul is free.
At four-score five, still stout and hale,
He heard a call to a farther trail;
So he turned his face where the stars are strewn;
"Elbowroom!" sighed Daniel Boone.

Down the Milky Way in its banks of blue
Far he has paddled his white canoe
To the splendid quest of the tameless soul —
He has reached the goal where there is no goal.
Now he rides and rides an endless trail
On the Hippogriff of the flaming tail
Or the Horse of the Stars with the golden mane,
As he rode the first of the blue-grass strain.
The joy that lies in the Search he seeks
On breathless hills with crystal peaks;

He makes his camp on heights untrod,
The steps of the Shrine, alone with God.
Through the woods of the vast, on the plains of Space
He hunts the pride of the Mammoth race
And the Dinosaur of the triple horn,
The manticore and Unicorn,
As once by the broad Missouri's flow
He followed the elk and the buffalo.
East of the Sun and west of the Moon,
"Elbowroom!" laughs Daniel Boone.

Arthur Guiterman

All One People

What did Hiamovi, the red man, Chief of the Cheyennes, have?
To a great chief at Washington and to a chief of peoples
    across the waters, Hiamovi spoke:
"There are birds of many colors — red, blue, green, yellow,
Yet it is all one bird.
There are horses of many colors — brown, black, yellow, white,
Yet it is all one horse.
So cattle, so all living things, animals, flowers, trees.
So men in this land, where once were only Indians, are
    now men of many colors — white, black, yellow, red.
Yet all one people.
That this should come to pass was in the heart of the
    Great Mystery.
It is right thus — and everywhere there shall be peace."
Thus Hiamovi, out of a tarnished and weatherworn heart
    of old gold, out of a living dawn gold.

Carl Sandburg

Excerpt from THE PEOPLE, YES by Carl Sandburg, copyright 1936 by Harcourt Brace Jovanovich, Inc.;
renewed 1964 by Carl Sandburg. Reprinted by permission of the publisher.

Original stone lithographs by Steve Forbis. NEW BUCKSKINS (opposite) and CROW PARADE (above).
Published by: NATIVE AMERICAN IMAGES, Box 746, Austin, Texas 78767. Print catalog available.

For You, O Democracy

Come, I will make the continent indissoluble,
I will make the most splendid race the sun ever shone upon.
I will make divine magnetic lands,
    With the love of comrades,
        With the life-long love of comrades.

I will plant companionship thick as trees along all the rivers
        of America, and along the shores of the great lakes,
        and all over the prairies,
I will make inseparable cities with their arms about each
        other's necks,
    By the love of comrades,
        By the manly love of comrades.

For you these from me, O Democracy, to serve you,
For you, for you I am trilling these songs.

Walt Whitman

Freedom

Where the mind is without fear and the head is held high;
Where knowledge is free;
Where the world has not been broken up into fragments
    by narrow domestic walls;
Where words come out from the depth of truth;
Where tireless striving stretches its arms towards
    perfection;
Where the clear stream of reason has not lost its way into
    the dreary desert sand of dead habit;
Where the mind is led forward by thee into ever-widening
    thought and action —
Into that heaven of freedom, my Father, let my country
    awake.

Rabindranath Tagore

Reprinted with permission of Macmillan Publishing Company from GITANJALI by Rabindranath Tagore (New York: Macmillan, 1913). Also by permission of Macmillan Press Ltd., London/Basingstoke.

Overleaf
SUNSET POINT
Bryce Canyon National Park
Grant Heilman Photography

JOHN MUIR

Praise for America's National Parks

MUIR WOODS

The poet's, commonly, is not a logger's path, but a woodman's. The logger and pioneer have preceded him, like John the Baptist; eaten the wild honey, it may be, but the locusts also; banished decaying wood and the spongy mosses which feed on it, and built hearths and humanized Nature for him.

But there are spirits of a yet more liberal culture, to whom no simplicity is barren. There are not only stately pines, but fragile flowers, like the orchises, commonly described as too delicate for cultivation, which derive their nutriment from the crudest mass of peat. These remind us, that, not only for strength, but for beauty, the poet must, from time to time, travel the logger's path and the Indian's trail, to drink at some new and more bracing fountain of the Muses, far in the recesses of the wilderness.

The kings of England formerly had their forests "to hold the king's game," for sport or food, sometimes destroying villages to create or extend them; and I think they were impelled by a true instinct. Why should not we, who have renounced the king's authority, have our national preserves, where no villages need be destroyed, in which the bear and panther, and some even of the hunter race, may still exist, and not be "civilized off the face of the earth," — our forests, not to hold the king's game merely, but to hold and preserve the king himself also, the lord of creation, — not for idle sport or food, but for inspiration and our own true recreation? Or shall we, like villains, grub them all up, poaching on our own national domains?

Henry David Thoreau
From *The Maine Woods*

YOSEMITE VALLEY

HALF DOME

YOSEMITE FALLS

Our elevation was now eleven thousand five hundred feet, and as the afternoon was less than half done, we had ample time to prepare beds, make tea, and gather a store of pitchy pine for our night fire. We chose the same camping ground I had selected two years before on the edge of a sedgy meadow enameled with buttercups and daisies, near a waterfall and snowbank, and surrounded with ranks of majestic alps. There were the withered pine tassels on which I had slept, and circling heap of stones built as a shelter from the downrushing night wind, and the remains of my woodpile gathered in case of a sudden snowstorm. Each made his own tin cupful of tea, and dinner was speedily accomplished. Then bed-building was vigorously carried on, each selecting willow shoots, pine tassels or withered grass with a zeal and naturalness whose sources must lie somewhere among our ancient grandfathers, when "wild in wood," etc. I have experimented with all kinds of plant pillows with especial reference to softness and fragrance, and here I was so happy as to invent a new one, composed of the leaves and flowers of the alpine shooting star, elastic, fragrant and truly beautiful. Here we rested as only mountaineers can. The wind fell to soft whispers, keen spiky shadows stole over the meadow, and pale and rosy light bathed the savage peaks, making a picture of Nature's repose that no words can ever describe. Darkness came, and the night wind began to flow like a deep and gentle river; the cascade nearby sounded all its notes with most impressive distinctness, and the sky glowed with living stars. Then came the moon, awakening the giant peaks that seemed to return her solemn gaze. The grand beauty of our chamber walls came out in wonderfully clear relief, white light and jet shadows revealing their wild fountain architecture, divested of all distracting details.

John Muir

EL CAPITAN

Steamboating! The Great American Adventure

"Sometimes we'd have that whole river all to ourselves for the longest time, and once or twice of a night we would see a steamboat slipping along in the dark...she would turn a corner and her lights would wink out...and leave the river still again...." Mark Twain

The Mississippi flows from the foothills of Minnesota to the jazz halls of New Orleans. Along the way, this mighty river is joined by the Ohio which winds westward from its source at the Allegheny and Monongahela Rivers. Mighty steamboats have traveled these waters since 1811 — the year the first grand paddlewheeler left Pittsburgh and traveled to New Orleans. This was the beginning of the Great Steamboat Era.

Steamboats, loaded with cotton and sugar cane, carried the pioneers, the traders, the planters, the businessmen, the lords and the ladies. At one point in time, more than 11,000 paddlewheelers plied these great rivers. Competition was fierce — so fierce that steamboats virtually became "floating palaces," each one trying to outdo the other.

Great European chefs created lavish banquets while the finest orchestras and riverboat musicians provided amusing entertainment. Guests enjoyed private bedrooms, named for various states and called staterooms. Crystal chandeliers, exquisite art pieces from all over the world, and rich mahogany and teakwork furnishings became the rule rather than the exception.

"Someday, they'll build the biggest steamboat the world has ever known; and she'll be long, white and gleaming in the sunshine with her twin black stacks. And that one shall be the Queen of the Mississippi." Mark Twain

If Mark Twain were alive today, he would see his dream rolling out of the early morning mist. He would hear the familiar sounds of riverboat tunes steaming from the Queen's giant calliope, the largest in the world. He would see her massive, two-story paddlewheel churning up a frothy wake. The magnificent Mississippi Queen is the largest steamboat ever built; yet her luxury and conveniences are beyond even Mark Twain's rich imagination.

"If cotton is king and surely he is, then the steamboat is the queen." Mark Twain

Excerpts from STEAMBOATIN' 1985 published by The Delta Queen Steamboat Co., Cincinnati, Ohio.

Photo opposite
MARK TWAIN
Artist Unknown
(Photo, Three Lions)

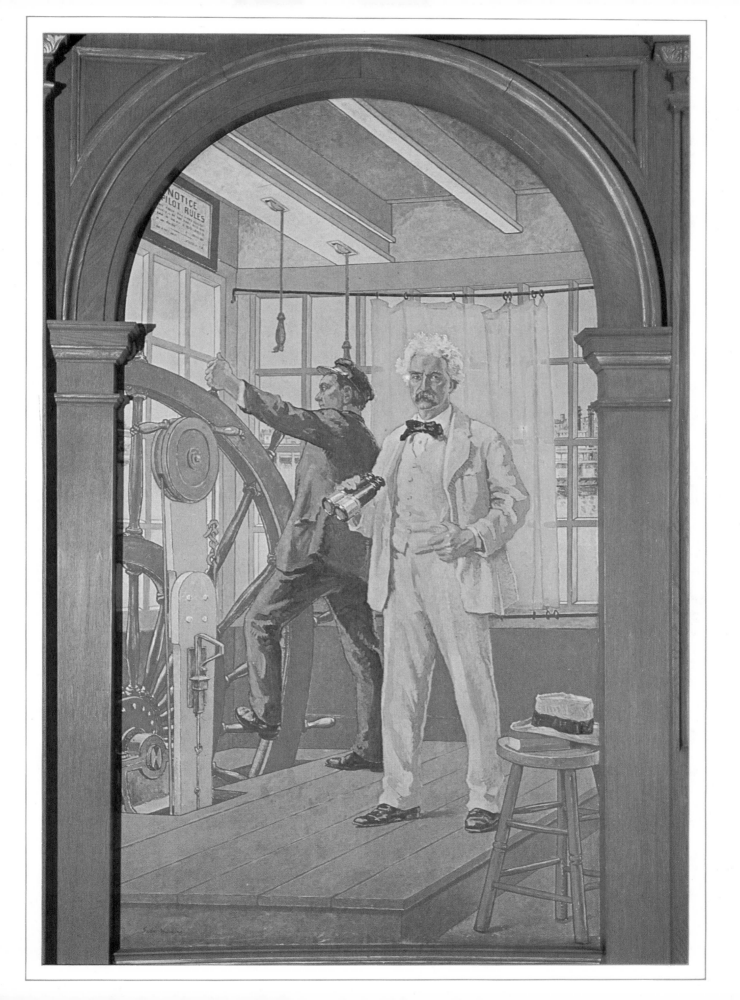

William F. Sparks

Editor's Note: Will Rogers (1879-1935), popular American humorist, radio commentator, and actor, was born November 4, 1879, at Oologah, Indian Territory (now Oklahoma). He began his career as a cowboy on the vaudeville stage but rose to wealth and world fame as a humorist and political commentator in the home-spun tradition of the old American frontier. Below are several of Rogers' politically-astute observations — in his personalized manner of spelling and speaking.

Will Rogers

Now, take George Washington — of course, he was great — he was the Father of our Country on account of having no children. He was a surveyor and he owned half of Virginia because he surveyed his own lines. He was a General on our side because England wouldent make him one of theirs. He was a politician and a gentleman — that is a rare combination.

The Capital was really the first real estate promotion scheme; Washington and Jefferson owned practically all the land down that way, and geographical reasons had nothing to do with locating the capital there. It wasent the center of the country, but it was the center of George's and Tom's land holdings. So while you dident get much money for being President in those days, it wasent exactly a philanthropic job. George lost no money through the transaction. He and Jefferson landed on two of the best hills in that country, and the Government got the swamps.

No man should ever make a speech after somebody has read or recited Lincoln's Gettysburg Address. It's only about 300 words long and the plainest words. There's not a child or even a comedian that can't understand it. Honest, Lincoln just as well not made his speech as far as it has had any effect on other speakers. He left it as an example but no one ever followed it.

What might be one classes "liberty" might be another classes "poison." Course, I guess absolute "Liberty" couldent mean anything but that anybody can do anything they want to do any time they want to. Well any half-wit can tell that wouldent work. So the question rises "How much liberty can you get and get away with it?" Well, you can get no more than you give. That's my definition, but you got perfect "Liberty" to work out your own, so get it.

Will Rogers quotations courtesy of Will Rogers Memorial, Claremore, Oklahoma.

American Flag

When Freedom from her mountain height
Unfurled her standard to the air,
She tore the azure robe of night,
And set the stars of glory there;
She mingled with its gorgeous dyes
The milky baldric of the skies,
And striped its pure, celestial white
With streakings of the morning light;
Then from his mansion in the sun
She called her eagle bearer down,
And gave into his mighty hand
The symbol of her chosen land.

Joseph Rodman Drake

Photo opposite
4TH OF JULY GREETINGS
Three Lions

GREETINGS OF 4TH JULY

George Washington

Only a baby, fair and small,
  Like many another baby son,
Whose smiles and tears come swift at call;
Who ate, and slept, and grew, that's all —
  The infant Washington.

Only a boy, like other boys,
  With tasks and studies, sports and fun;
Fond of his books and games and toys;
Living his childish griefs and joys —
  The little Washington.

Only a lad, awkward and shy,
  Skilled in handling a horse or gun;
Mastering knowledge that, by and by,
Should aid him in duties great and high —
  The youthful Washington.

Only a man of finest bent,
  Hero of battles fought and won;
Surveyor, General, President,
Who served his country, and died content —
  The patriot Washington.

Only — ah! what was the secret, then,
  Of his being America's honored son?
Why was he famed above other men?
His name upon every tongue and pen —
  The illustrious Washington.

A mighty brain, a will to endure,
  Passions subdued, a slave to none,
A heart that was brave and strong and sure,
A soul that was noble and great and pure,
A faith in God that was held secure —
  This was George Washington.

Author Unknown

AMONG DAKOTA'S HILLS

No crumbling stone — no mellow rock
   The sculptor seeks where to reveal
The foremost men of hardy stock
   Who served their country with rare zeal.

Among Dakota's hills so grand
   The storms of time that never cease
Touch lightly mighty crags that stand
   Where Borglum carves his masterpiece!

What if stone is a toilsome page?
   How could a truly mindful son
Forget in this the golden age
   The blessings the brave fathers won?

Look up, all you patriots true!
   Where once the bare rock outward spread,
There valiant men have come in view.
   Their deeds still live — they are not dead.

Our Washington warns of foreign foe,
   Who would assail our shores again;
While Jefferson would have us know
   That tyrants rise 'mongst thoughtless men.

Our Lincoln pleads for greater faith
   In boundless power of the right
To hold intact the Ship of State,
   And overcome opposing might.

There's Roosevelt who could inspire
   His fellow man to seek high goals,
And hold to a wholesome desire,
   And not to plead for grants and doles.

O Carver of the Noble Brow,
   Hath ever other dreamer known
Such inspiration as yours now
   To carve life into lifeless stone?

Frank Manhart

Photo opposite
MOUNT RUSHMORE
South Dakota
H. Armstrong Roberts

The Gettysburg Address

Fourscore and seven years ago our fathers brought forth on this continent a new nation, conceived in liberty, and dedicated to the proposition that all men are created equal. Now we are engaged in a great civil war, testing whether that nation, or any nation so conceived and so dedicated, can long endure. We are met on a great battle-field of that war. We have come to dedicate a portion of that field as a final resting-place for those who here gave their lives that that nation might live. It is altogether fitting and proper that we should do this. But, in a larger sense, we cannot dedicate — we cannot consecrate — we cannot hallow — this ground. The brave men, living and dead, who struggled here, have consecrated it far above our poor power to add or detract. The world will little note nor long remember what we say here, but it can never forget what they did here. It is for us, the living, rather, to be dedicated here to the unfinished work which they who fought here have thus far so nobly advanced. It is rather for us to be here dedicated to the great task remaining before us — that from these honored dead we take increased devotion to that cause for which they gave the last full measure of devotion; that we here highly resolve that these dead shall not have died in vain; that this nation, under God, shall have a new birth of freedom; and that government of the people, by the people, for the people, shall not perish from the earth.

Abraham Lincoln

— November 19, 1863

The New Colossus

Not like the brazen giant of Greek fame,
With conquering limbs astride from land to land;
Here at our sea-washed sunset gates shall stand
A mighty woman with a torch, whose flame
Is the imprisoned lightning, and her name
Mother of Exiles. From her beacon-hand
Glows world-wide welcome; her mild eyes command
The air-bridged harbor that twin-cities frame.
"Keep, ancient lands, your storied pomp!" cries she
With silent lips. "Give me your tired, your poor,
Your huddled masses yearning to breathe free,
The wretched refuse of your teeming shore.
Send these, the homeless, tempest-tossed to me —
I lift my lamp beside the golden door!"

Emma Lazarus

Photo opposite
STATUE OF LIBERTY
H. Armstrong Roberts

The Star★Spangled Banner

A Standardized version of the melody

Words by
Francis Scott Key
(1779-1843)

Music by
John Stafford Smith
(1750-1838)
Harmonized by
Walter Damrosch

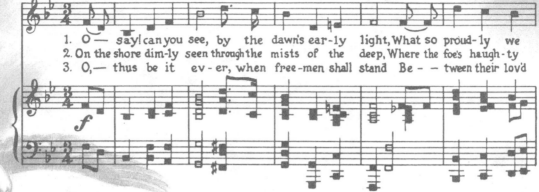

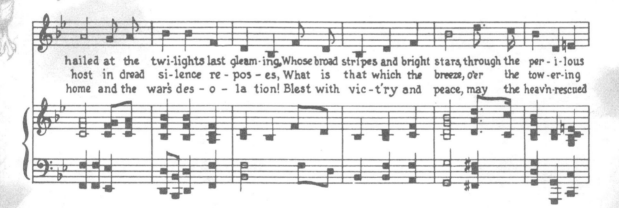

1. O— say! can you see, by the dawn's ear-ly light, What so proud-ly we
2. On the shore dim-ly seen through the mists of the deep, Where the foe's haugh-ty
3. O,— thus be it ev-er, when free-men shall stand Be——tween their lov'd

hailed at the twi-lights last gleam-ing, Whose broad stripes and bright stars, through the per-i-lous
host in dread si-lence re-pos-es, What is that which the breeze, o'er the tow-er-ing
home and the war's des-o-la tion! Blest with vic-t'ry and peace, may the heav'n-rescued

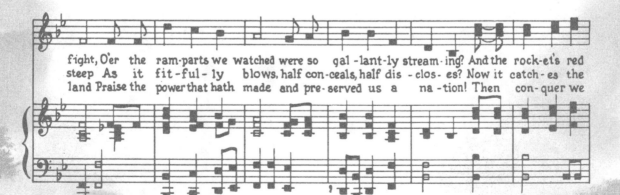

fight, O'er the ram-parts we watched were so gal-lant-ly stream-ing? And the rock-et's red
steep As it fit-ful-ly blows, half con-ceals, half dis-clos-es? Now it catch-es the
land Praise the power that hath made and pre-served us a na-tion! Then con-quer we

glare, the bombs burst-ing in air Gave proof through the night that our flag was still
gleam of the morn-ing's first beam, In full glo-ry re-flect-ed now shines on the
must, when our cause it is just, And this be our mot-to-"In God is our

there. O— say, does that Star-Span-gled Ban-ner yet
stream. 'Tis the Star-Span-gled Ban-ner— O, long may it
Trust." And the Star-Span-gled Ban-ner in tri-umph shall

wave— O'er the land— of the free and the home of the brave?
wave— O'er the land— of the free and the home of the brave!
wave— O'er the land— of the free and the home of the brave.

The Attic of America

I am the Smithsonian. I am the world in microcosm — an attic where the children and grandchildren of this land may seek and find their dreams.

Like the first citizens of this country, I was conceived across the sea. Originally the offspring of an English nobleman, I became naturalized and thoroughly Americanized. James Smithson would be proud to see his dream of "an establishment for the increase and diffusion of knowledge among men." I am that dream. I am reality. I am the Smithsonian. I am more than buildings and architecture, more than science and art. I am the ridiculous and the sublime, a mirror and an image.

I am antiquity. Here you may pass from the summer brightness of a Washington afternoon into a dimly lit cave to witness a Neanderthal burial. See the widow and her orphaned son mourn their tens-of-thousands-year-old loss and sense the anguish fresh as yesterday.

I am tomorrow. Walk the moon and share the exhilaration of a NASA cruise. Pierce the universe and peel the layered mysteries from distant planets.

I am beauty. Wonder at the ethereal hues as light dances across a fragile Chinese moth. Trace the fluid marble of a sculpted angel's wing.

I am priceless. For on my shelves and in my secret places you will find jewels and golden relics from the treasuries of kings. My columns guard the works of Copley, Whistler, Homer and Cassatt.

But I am commonplace as well — an ice cream parlor chair, some boxing gloves, a campaign button, a carousel. For these are part of us, of life, and this is what I am.

I am the history of America. Here all the first ladies silently parade by in gowns of myriad hue and style. A continental gunboat, dredged from the frigid depths of Lake Champlain, rests in my halls. And here you will find our first president's teeth and Roosevelt's teddy bear. For history is bits and pieces, not just broad tableaus.

I am the living. Stroll the zoo and visit rare pandas munching on bamboo. Watch white tigers nap and monkeys romp and lovely liquid reptiles twine around a tree.

I am a local resident, dwelling within the boundaries of our nation's capital. My origins rest on Independence Avenue, housed in a Norman castle built of red sandstone in 1855. Since then I've grown from one to fourteen buildings. Each reflects the unique diversity of this varied land. My National Museum of Natural History stands in grandeur behind Corinthian columns. The Hirshhorn, a forbidding concrete cylinder 82 feet high and 231 feet in diameter, guards my treasures of art and sculpture. But not far away, the glass and gray stone edifice of the Air and Space Museum salutes the contemporary inspiration of its architects. And on they go — each building individual, yet each part of a whole.

Although my body rests at home, my spirit always moves. My researchers and scientists may be in Sri Lanka or the Arctic. My equipment and technicians might be fording rivers in Brazil, seeking, searching, gathering, gambling, bringing home the sights and sounds, the textures of the world.

I am all things to each. A child might know his first glimpse of his past inside my doors. A young man dreams his first dream of a flight to outer space. Where else could wizened codgers sit and reminisce with evidence to prove their memories true?

I am not forgotten relics stored on long forgotten shelves. I am the attic of America: the treasure boxes all the children of this country may explore.

Pamela Kennedy

Photo opposite
THE SMITHSONIAN INSTITUTION
Ed Cooper

Gail Brook Burket

Gail Brook Burket wrote her first poem when she was eight years old and has been writing ever since. This author of eight books, numerous articles, and several hundred poems is a member of prestigious literary societies, including the Poetry Society of America and The National League of American Pen Women.

Some of Mrs. Burket's poems have been set to music. She and her late husband, Dr. Walter Cleveland Burket, a distinguished surgeon who composed music, sent an original Christmas carol to their friends each year for forty-three years. Two of her religious poems were included as hymns in *American Hymns Old and New*, published by Columbia University Press in 1980.

Mrs. Burket's inspirational poetry has appeared in many *Ideals* issues throughout the years.

High in the Mountains

High in the mountains the mornings come
With a grandiose roll of the sun's gold drum.
High in the mountains the days march by
With flamboyant blue banners of shining sky.

High in the mountains a listener hears
The mystical melody of the spheres.
Nightly the minstrel old winds will croon
To the lilting notes of the stars and moon.

High in the mountains the folks are wise,
For a dream is kept lighted in mountain eyes.
Fun is their neighbor and care their foe,
And their love ever deepens as valleys grow.

High in the mountains there is joy to share
With the loneliest stranger who wanders there.
Beauty and strength glow without and within,
For the mountains and people are kith and kin.

Sing, America, Sing

Take up your harp, America,
This is the hour for song.
Let myriad-throated harmony
Rise jubilant and strong.

Forward, invincible with song,
Loved homeland of the free.
With mighty steps and mighty songs,
Achieve your destiny.

A singing nation can prevail
Against the strongest foe.
A singing people marches on,
Undaunted as they go.

Then sweep the strings with valiant song,
Let hill and valley ring.
Lift up your hearts and voices, all
America, and sing!

The People

This land, whose founders cherished liberty,
Produced a people venturesome and strong,
With kindness as untrammeled as the sea,
Keen, homespun humor and contempt for wrong.
Their ax blades rang, their rough-hewn plows cut straight
Across the sod. They sowed their lives like seed
Into the nation they envisioned great,
Resolved to make their dream accomplished deed.

From the four corners of the world they came
To build the new republic which would rise
In startling splendor, like a comet's flame,
Whose sudden brilliance floods the star-strewn skies.
They left a heritage by life and death:
The land where freedom breathed her first pure breath.

Song for Young Americans

I live in a land
Where the people are free
And joy is a birthright
Belonging to me.
Love shelters my home
Like a wide-branching tree.
The doors of the church
Are open to me.
The schools unlock treasure
With truth for a key.
A whole world of wonder
Is waiting for me.
I live in a land
Where the people are free;
The future shines golden
For children like me.

To Americans

They chose a pioneer's harsh life: strange land,
Cold, loneliness, a rough-hewn cabin home,
And blood-marked trails worn deep across grim sand,
High hostile peaks, and rutted prairie loam.
A dream led them, a dream undreamed before;
A dream of people unafraid and free.
From many nations, ancient scars, and war,
They wrought a new triumphant unity.

We will not disavow their dream. We stand
With eager faces turned toward future days,
Ready to march ahead until our land
Has reached the heights by yet untraveled ways.
United, old in wisdom, young in might,
We bear the living flame of freedom's light.

American Favorite

American as corn on the cob,
Perennial as a picket fence,
As right as rain, when dust is deep,
And down to earth as common sense,

A freshly baked apple pie exudes
Enticing flavors from each slice,
Whose flaky crust and luscious fruit
Fling tantalizing whiffs of spice.

Parfait, cake, pudding or meringue
Cannot compete with juicy wedges
Of crisp brown pastry, flaunting frills
Of apple goodness on the edges.

Disneyland: Tribute to America

Walter Elias Disney exemplified all that is best in America. Combining far-reaching vision and bold initiative with Yankee ingenuity and industry, he was living proof of the American Dream in action.

Walt was born in Chicago in 1901. The youngest of four boys, he learned the meaning of responsibility and hard work early in his childhood. His father, Elias, moved his family around the Midwest trying his hand at various trades — construction, farming and a newspaper delivery service — and he expected his sons to pitch in and help.

Money was often tight in the Disney household but Walt's parents made sure there was enough for art classes. They knew how much Walt loved drawing. World War I sidetracked his enthusiasm, however, when at sixteen he enlisted as a Red Cross ambulance driver in France. But when Walt returned home in 1919 he turned to art once more, working first for a local art studio, and then for a company which made animated theater commercials.

These jobs gave Walt the experience and money to form his own small cartoon studio, Laugh-O-Grams. Walt worked tirelessly, but he was not able to get back the time and money he'd invested in producing the cartoons and he was forced to close the studio. Never one to give up though, he moved to Los Angeles and gradually built up another studio there. In 1928, the company released "Steamboat Willie." The cartoon featured film's newest technological advancement — sound — and a loveable mouse named Mickey, who captivated audiences and critics alike.

As the celebrated mouse's fame and success grew so did the scope and reputation of the Disney studio. In the following years, the Disney team produced such classics as "The Three Little Pigs," "Fantasia," "Dumbo," "Mary Poppins," and "Jungle Book."

Having reached the top in films, Walt now searched for new challenges. He envisioned a playground of vast and myriad wonders for both children and adults. Disneyland would serve to remind the world of past achievements and would pay tribute to Yankee technological ingenuity.

Walt was not able to find financial backers for this ambitious project. Undeterred, he sold his vacation home and borrowed against his insurance policies. He was never to regret the gamble. After many struggles by a team of highly-skilled professionals led by Walt, Disneyland opened in California in 1955.

Not content to rest on his laurels, Disney was already looking ahead to his last and greatest creative milestone — Walt Disney World. Tragically, he was never to see that dream become reality. He died on December 15, 1966, just over a year after purchasing the park's site in Florida, before he was able to complete his "showcase to the world for the ingenuity and imagination of American free enterprise."

But his dreams lived on, and in October, 1982, Epcot Center, the second phase of Walt Disney World, opened. Epcot echoes Disney's lifelong faith and trust in the continued greatness of humanity. It provides an inspiring forum where people from all over the world can gather together in an atmosphere of celebration and goodwill to share in each other's technological advances, uniqueness and richness. Epcot remains a worthy tribute to the man who dared to dream his dreams on a large scale and possessed the foresight, ambition, boldness and determination to realize them, not only for his benefit, but for the benefit of all.

Nayda Rondon

Photo opposite
THE MAGIC CASTLE
Lawrence Mooney
Cyr Color Photo Agency

Readers' Reflections

I Stood Beside the Flag Today

I stood beside the flag today
And watched it gently wave;
I saw amidst the stars and stripes
America, the great...

A land to which the masses turn,
A land that still is free,
A country that still has been spared
The rule of tyranny.

I stood beside the grand old flag,
The tried red, white and blue...
Compatriots, this flag and I,
Of a nation fair to view.

A nation built upon God's truth,
Where He is still the key
To keeping this, our glorious land,
A torch of liberty.

Loise Pinkerton Fritz

Washington and Lincoln

In our little schoolhouse
High upon the wall,
Washington and Lincoln
Oversaw us all.

Did they hear our lessons?
Did they blame or bless
When we missed a question,
Made a second guess?

Time has passed and memory
Serves the fleeting years,
Sometimes fraught with laughter,
Oft times touched with tears.

Still we see their vigil
As we oft recall
Washington and Lincoln
On our schoolroom wall.

Minnie Klemme

Editor's Note: Readers are invited to submit poetry, short anecdotes, and humorous reflections on life for possible publication in future Ideals issues. Writers will receive $10 for each published submission. Send material to "Readers' Reflections," P.O. Box 1101, Milwaukee, Wisconsin 53201.

Old New Salem

The grass grows green in old Salem Park,
And the trees around are cool and dark.
The wind blows softly as it used to do
When Lincoln was young and the town was new.

Here is the store where he went to work
As a splitter of rails and a part-time clerk.
In the little back room were his chair and his bed,
With a candle nearby, and the books he read.

Here is the shop of Lincoln's friend,
With its cooper's tools, and the fire in the end
Where Lincoln stretched out and read by the light
Of the cooper's shavings, there in the night.

Across the silence echoes laughter,
The kind that used to follow after
Young Abe Lincoln's famous jokes
With all those denim-clad pioneer folks.

Across the years flash the smiles and the tears
Of the pioneer folk with their joys and their fears
As a fiddler starts a foot-stamping tune,
And an old hound dog turns and bays at the moon.

The Rutledge Tavern is tranquil and gray,
But it used to be noisy, and busy, and gay
When Lincoln and young Ann, the love of his life,
Planned for their future as man and wife.

They loved each other, and walked hand-in-hand
To the edge of the village, and there the land
Stretched out where the Sangamon River was running,
And wary-eyed wolves were cautiously sunning.

The grass grows green in old Salem Park,
And the trees around are cool and dark.
The wind blows softly, as it used to do,
When Lincoln was young, and the town was new.

Virginia Prichard Murphy

Overleaf
THE "GAZELA PRIMEIRO"
Penn's Landing, Philadelphia
H. Armstrong Roberts

O Beautiful, My Country

O beautiful, my country!
   Be thine a nobler care,
Than all thy wealth of commerce,
   Thy harvest waving fair;
Be it thy pride to lift up
   The manhood of the poor;
Be thou to the oppressed
   Fair Freedom's open door.

For thee our fathers suffered,
   For thee they toiled and prayed;
Upon thy holy altar
   Their willing lives they laid.
Thou hast no common birthright;
   Grand memories on thee shine,
The blood of pilgrim nations,
   Commingled, flows in thine.

O beautiful, our country!
   Round thee in love we draw;
Thine is the grace of freedom,
   The majesty of law.
Be righteousness thy scepter,
   Justice thy diadem;
And on thy shining forehead
   Be peace the crowning gem.

Frederick L. Hosmer

From THE THOUGHT OF GOD by Frederick L. Hosmer and William C. Gannett. Copyright 1918 by Beacon Press. Reprinted by permission of Beacon Press.

America The Beautiful

O beautiful for spacious skies,
  For amber waves of grain,
For purple mountain majesties
  Above the fruited plain!
    America! America!
  God shed His grace on thee
And crown thy good with brotherhood
  From sea to shining sea!

O beautiful for pilgrim feet,
  Whose stern, impassioned stress
A thoroughfare for freedom beat
  Across the wilderness!
    America! America!
  God mend thine every flaw,
Confirm thy soul in self-control,
  Thy liberty in law!

O beautiful for patriot dream
  That sees beyond the years
Thine alabaster cities gleam
  Undimmed by human tears!
    America! America!
  God shed His grace on thee
And crown thy good with brotherhood
  From sea to shining sea!

Katharine Lee Bates

America's Welcome Home

Oh, gallantly they fared forth in khaki and in blue,
America's crusading host of warriors bold and true;
They battled for the rights of men beside our brave Allies,
And now they're coming home to us with glory in their eyes.

Oh, it's home again, and home again, America for me!
Our hearts are turning home again and there we long to be,
In our beautiful big country beyond the ocean bars,
Where the air is full of sunlight and the flag is full of stars.

They bore our country's great word across the rolling sea,
"America swears brotherhood with all the just and free."
They wrote that word victorious on fields of mortal strife,
And many a valiant lad was proud to seal it with his life.

Oh, welcome home in Heaven's peace, dear spirits of the dead!
And welcome home ye living sons America hath bred!
The lords of war are beaten down, your glorious task is done;
You fought to make the whole world free, and the victory is won.

Now it's home again, and home again, our hearts are turning west,
Of all the lands beneath the sun America is best.
We're going home to our own folks, beyond the ocean bars,
Where the air is full of sunlight and the flag is full of stars.

Henry van Dyke

Henry van Dyke, "America's Welcome Home" from THE POEMS OF HENRY VAN DYKE. Copyright 1920 by Charles Scribner's Sons; copyright renewed 1948 Charles Scribner's Sons. Reprinted with the permission of Charles Scribner's Sons.

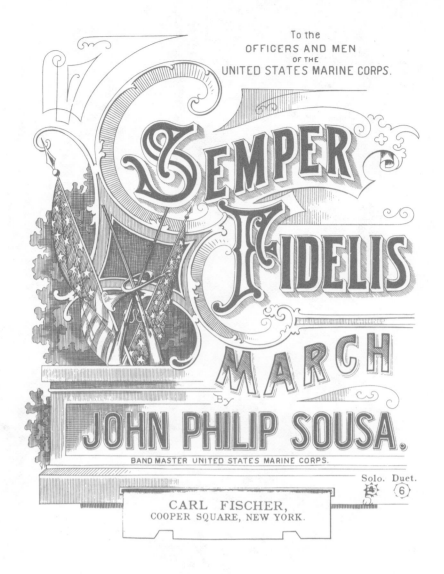

To the
OFFICERS AND MEN
OF THE
UNITED STATES MARINE CORPS.

Semper Fidelis
MARCH
BY
JOHN PHILIP SOUSA.
BAND MASTER UNITED STATES MARINE CORPS.

Solo. Duet.
6

CARL FISCHER,
COOPER SQUARE, NEW YORK.

Stars and Stripes
Forever
SONG.

By JOHN PHILIP SOUSA.

PUBLISHED BY
THE JOHN CHURCH COMPANY
CINCINNATI   NEW YORK   CHICAGO   LEIPSIC

HAIL TO
THE SPIRIT OF LIBERTY
MARCH
BY JOHN PHILIP SOUSA

SEMPER FIDELIS
MARCH

By John Philip Sousa

The Torch Is Passed

The world is very different now. For man holds in his mortal hands the power to abolish all forms of human poverty and all forms of human life. And yet the same revolutionary beliefs for which our forebearers fought are still at issue around the globe — the belief that the rights of man come not from the generosity of the state but from the hand of God.

We dare not forget today that we are the heirs of that first revolution. Let the word go forth from this time and place, to friend and foe alike, that the torch has been passed to a new generation of Americans — born in this century, tempered by war, disciplined by a hard and bitter peace, proud of our ancient heritage — and unwilling to witness or permit the slow undoing of those human rights to which this nation has always been committed, and to which we are committed today at home and around the world.

Let every nation know, whether it wishes us well or ill, that we shall pay any price, bear any burden, meet any hardship, support any friend, oppose any foe to assure the survival and the success of liberty . . . .

In the long history of the world, only a few generations have been granted the role of defending freedom in its hour of maximum danger. I do not shrink from this responsibility — I welcome it. I do not believe that any of us would exchange places with any other people or any other generation. The energy, the faith, the devotion which we bring to this endeavor will light our country and all who serve it — and the glow from that fire can truly light the world.

And so, my fellow Americans: ask not what your country can do for you — ask what you can do for your country.

My fellow citizens of the world: ask not what America will do for you, but what together we can do for the freedom of man.

Finally, whether you are citizens of America or citizens of the world, ask of us here the same high standards of strength and sacrifice which we ask of you. With a good conscience our only sure reward, with history the final judge of our deeds, let us go forth to lead the land we love, asking His blessing and His help, but knowing that here on earth God's work must truly be our own.

John F. Kennedy

—January 20, 1961

Photo opposite
AIR FORCE ACADEMY
Colorado Springs
Richard Carkeek
Cyr Color Photo Agency

Night Journey

Now as the train bears west,
Its rhythm rocks the earth,
And from my Pullman berth
I stare into the night
While others take their rest.
Bridges of iron lace,
A suddenness of trees,
A lap of mountain mist
All cross my line of sight,
Then a bleak wasted place,
And a lake below my knees.
Full on my neck I feel
The straining at a curve;
My muscles move with steel,
I wake in every nerve.
I watch a beacon swing
From dark to blazing bright;
We thunder through ravines
And gullies washed with light.
Beyond the mountain pass
Mist deepens on the pane;
We rush into a rain
That rattles double glass.
Wheels shake the roadbed stone,
The pistons jerk and shove,
I stay up half the night
To see the land I love.

Theodore Roethke

From the book THE COLLECTED POEMS OF THEODORE ROETHKE by Theodore Roethke.
Copyright © 1953 by Theodore Roethke. "Night Journey" Copyright © 1940 by Theodore
Roethke. Published by Doubleday and Co., Inc.

A New Frontier

These lines recall how NASA's team
Began fulfillment of a dream:
A trek in space beyond the sky
Where realms of unseen wonder lie.
In February 'sixty-two
An Atlas Missile pierced the blue.

Designers, builders, engineers
Prepared this thrust for three long years.
Despite delays in scheduled flights,
Experts patiently set their sights
To send a spacecraft round the earth
In paths of predetermined girth.

With complex systems all OK
Finally dawned the lift-off day.
In U.S.A.'s bold tradition
Countdown experts boomed, "Ignition!"
Bell-shaped capsule Friendship Seven
Broke earth's bonds on try eleven.

Since that first successful mission
Others have pursued the vision:
Brave-hearted astro-pioneers
Explore for us new space frontiers.
Like Glenn, they seek God's strength and light
To use those hard-earned space wings right.

Joseph Hughes Hartough

Photo opposite
APOLLO 14
Cape Kennedy, Florida
Bill Lees
Cyr Color Photo Agency

Sail On, O Ship of State

Thou, too, sail on, O Ship of State!
Sail on, O Union, strong and great!
Humanity with all its fears,
With all its hopes of future years,
Is hanging breathless on thy fate!
We know what Master laid thy keel,
What workmen wrought thy ribs of steel,
Who made each mast, and sail, and rope,
What anvils rang, what hammers beat,
In what a forge and what a heat
Were shaped the anchors of thy hope!
Fear not each sudden sound and shock,
'Tis of the wave and not the rock;
'Tis but the flapping of the sail,
And not a rent made by the gale!
In spite of rock and tempest's roar,
In spite of false lights on the shore,
Sail on, nor fear to breast the sea!
Our hearts, our hopes, are all with thee,
Our hearts, our hopes, our prayers, our tears,
Our faith, triumphant o'er our fears,
Are all with thee — are all with thee!

Henry Wadsworth Longfellow

Ideals Welcomes Springtime!

We invite you to share with us the joyous message of Easter and the reawakening of spring in our next issue, Easter Ideals.

Marvel at a beautiful depiction of the traditional Easter story; learn the art of Easter egg decoupage; delight in the recollection of a most unusual Easter Parade.

All of this — and much more — accompanied by outstanding color photography and original artwork.

Give a beautiful and on-going gift to family and friends — an Ideals subscription, beginning with our Easter issue.

ACKNOWLEDGMENTS

AMERICA THE BEAUTIFUL from POEMS by Katharine Lee Bates, E. P. Dutton Publishers; SING, AMERICA, SING and TO AMERICANS by Gail Brook Burket from ONE THOUSAND AMERICAN THINGS, copyright 1949 and 1956 by The Spencer Press, Inc.; THE NEW NATION from A BALLAD OF THE BOSTON TEA PARTY in THE COMPLETE POETICAL WORKS OF OLIVER WENDELL HOLMES, copyright 1908 by Houghton Mifflin Company; THE NEW COLOSSUS from THE POEMS OF EMMA LAZARUS, Vol. I, 1889; AMONG DAKOTA'S HILLS from THE CLAN AND OTHER POEMS, copyright 1953 by Frank J. Manhart, Hill House Press Publishers, Richmond, Virginia, reprinted with permission; the selection from THE NEW WORLD by Edgar Lee Masters, copyright 1937 by D. Appleton & Co.; our sincere thanks to the following authors whose addresses we were unable to locate: Harry Brown for the selection from THE POEM OF BUNKER HILL taken from THE POETRY OF FREEDOM, copyright 1945 by Random House Publishers; and Frederic R. Gunsky for CAMPING ON THE MOUNTAIN by John Muir from SOUTH OF YOSEMITE, edited and copyrighted © 1968 by Frederic R. Gunsky.

Statement of ownership, management and circulation (Required by 39 U.S.C. 3685), of IDEALS, published 8 times a year in Feb.; Mar.; May; June; Aug.; Sept.; Nov.; Dec. at Milwaukee, Wisconsin for September 1984. Publisher, Ideals Publishing Corporation; Editor, Kathleen S. Pohl; Managing Editor, Marybeth Owens; Owner, Thomas Nelson, Inc., Nelson Place at Elm Hill Pike, P. O. Box 141000, Nashville, Tennessee 37214. The known bondholders, mortgagees, and other security holders owning or holding 1 percent or more of total amount of bonds, mortgages or other securities are: None. Average no. copies each issue during preceding 12 months: Total no. copies printed (Net Press Run) 221,157. Paid circulation 39,538. Mail subscriptions 166,405. Total paid circulation 205,943. Free distribution 363. Total distribution 206,306. Actual no. copies of single issue published nearest to filing date: Total no. copies printed (Net Press Run) 180,586. Paid circulation 9,363. Other sales 163,885. Free distribution 41. Total distribution 173,289. I certify that the statements made by me are correct and complete. Donald A. Gottschalk, President.